Online Traffic Unlimited

Ranking Secrets

[O. Addey]

Copyright © 2021 ***O. Addey***

All rights reserved.

Table of Contents

Introduction 7

Chapter-01: Website Traffic: Recap 8

    What is Traffic? 8

    What's the distinction between bandwidth and traffic? 8

    Why does traffic cost money? 9

    What is unlimited traffic? 9

    How much traffic will I need? 10

Chapter-02: Increase Traffic to Your Website 11

    Advertise 11

    Get Social 11

    Write Irresistible Headlines 12

    Target Long-Tail Keywords 12

    Start Guest Blogging 13

    Go After Referral Traffic 13

    Implement Schema Microdata 14

    Link Internally 14

    Interview Industry Thought Leaders 15

    Make Sure Your Site is Responsive 15

    Make Sure Your Site is Fast 15

    Foster a Sense of Community 16

Make Yourself Heard in Comment Sections 16

Examine Your Analytics Data 17

Submit Your Content to Aggregator Sites............ 17

Incorporate Video into Your Content Strategy 18

Host Webinars 18

Attend Conferences 18

Chapter-03: Other Free Ways to Increase Website Traffic... 20

Get Listed in Online Directories 20

Build Backlinks 20

Post to Social Media 21

Include Hashtags in Your Posts 21

Use Landing Pages 22

Start Email Marketing 22

Guest Blog 23

Learn from Your Analytics 23

Chapter-04: Paid Methods of Generating Website Traffic... 24

Social Media Advertising 24

Display Advertising 24

Avoid Instant Website Traffic Generators 25

Automatic Website Traffic Generators Can Be Harmful to Your Rankings 25

Your traffic Won't Be Targeted 25

Your Site Could Get Banned 25

Google Paid Ways to Drive Website Traffic 26

Google Ads 26

Google Maps Advertising............................. 27

Chapter-05: Increase Website Traffic from Google . 28

Why More Website Traffic? 28

Free Traffic vs. Quality Traffic 28

Quality Traffic Driven Channels to Your Website . 29

Optimize Your Free Google Business Profile 30

Your Google listing 30

Keep in mind, too, that Google My Business: .. 30

Perform On-Page SEO 31

Chapter-06: Increase Website Traffic via social media 32

Start a podcast.. 32

Write on Medium 32

Master YouTube marketing 33

Increase website traffic with LinkedIn 33

Add social share buttons 34

Engage in email marketing 34
Maximize Twitter marketing 34
Check out Pinterest 35
Try influencer marketing 35
Reach out to affiliates 36
Advertise via ad networks 36
Optimize your best traffic source 37
Conclusion 38

Introduction

Increasing website traffic is a common objective among many business owners and marketers, whether you own an e-commerce store or a brick-and-mortar store. Your website functions as an online store where visitors learn more about your services, develop confidence in your brand, and ultimately become leads and customers. However, having a nice, easy-to-navigate website will not result in more consumers if no one can discover it in the first place. Here you will learn how to be noticed online so that you can optimize your visibility. Many of us are aware that SEO may be an excellent technique to drive visitors to a website. However, search engine optimization may be our sole way of increasing traffic and search results for some of us. You must learn how to diversify traffic to your website and not rely just on search engine optimization. Otherwise, if your major traffic source fails, your firm may be doomed. We'll have to look at how you may boost website and blog post traffic without relying just on SEO. We'll look at several methods that you can implement right now and maximize each source of traffic. If you ask a marketer or a business owner what they want most in the world, they will almost certainly respond, "More customers." What is frequently placed after customers on a company's wish list?

Chapter-01: Website Traffic: Recap

What is Traffic?

When someone visits your website on the internet, web pages, pictures, and other data are downloaded to their computer. The majority of corporate websites send 1GB to 5GB of data each month. Monthly traffic is the highest quantity of data transfer your site may deliver in a given month without exceeding the plan's restrictions. Most businesses should never have to worry about traffic because we give a sufficient number of free transfers per month based on your plan. After the first 1GB of extra Traffic, a configurable sliding scale kicks in, and dedicated servers are available for up to 300GB.

What's the distinction between bandwidth and traffic?

Many businesses use the term bandwidth to describe their traffic constraints. The breadth of the conduit through which data passes is referred to as its bandwidth. The volume of data delivered and received, on the other hand, is referred to as traffic. A 56kbps modem, for example, can transport 56,000 bits (7kb) per second. Therefore, the modem has a 56kbps bandwidth. Although your workplace ADSL connection may provide 256Kbps-24Mbps bandwidth, your monthly traffic limit maybe 6GD. Many hosting providers give 1Mbps or 10Mbps internet connections per server. We are linked to our upstream supplier via several 1Gbps lines connected to various fiber connections totaling over 4Tbps (4000Gbps+) of internet bandwidth.

Why does traffic cost money?

Due to the expenses of maintaining national and international communications infrastructure and cabling, all internet users, including ISPs, are paid for internet traffic. Large telecommunications firms that operate telecommunications networks, like us, pass maintenance costs on to their consumers. This is why foreign phone calls are more expensive or have per-minute charges and why your home ADSL connection has a monthly bandwidth restriction. Unfortunately, in comparison to other nations, traffic prices in Australia are extremely high. However, our network speeds are often faster, with 1Gb lines to our data centers instead of the 1Mb or 10Mb links commonly provided by overseas hosting companies (they might not mention that on their websites).

What is unlimited traffic?

Some hosting companies (particularly in the United States) disregard their bandwidth limits and install thousands of websites on the same servers and connections.

Alternatively, they may restrict your server to a one or 2Mbps connection, with realistic transfer rates far less than the 200GB/month they advertise in their plans. This overloads the connections, causing the majority of your consumers to wait longer than necessary. Slow connections are especially evident during busy periods - imagine you've just been Slashdotted or mentioned in the media. When you require the most power and traffic, your site becomes inaccessible. It's bad for businesses and for developers who want to be known for their talents or publications. Our load-ratio rules and scalability keep both our customers and your customers happy. Some servers will even disconnect you if your site becomes too busy, citing "over-usage of CPU cycles," and require you to upgrade before you can access your site again. As a result, while the plan may state "Unlimited Traffic," it is restricted by connection speed, server speed, and the provider's concealed "true restriction."

How much traffic will I need?

Assume your site receives 1000 visitors per month, and each visitor receives 3-4 pages of text and graphics (about 400k) with no caching. 1000 visits multiplied by 400KB equals 400,000KB = 400MB each month. In this instance, your site would require at least 400-500MB of Traffic each month.

Chapter-02: Increase Traffic to Your Website

Advertise

This one is so clear that we'll start with it. Paid search, social media marketing, and display advertising are excellent methods for generating visits, establishing your brand, and getting your website in front of people. First, tailor your paid techniques to your goals - do you merely want more visits, or do you also want to increase conversions? Each sponsored channel has advantages and downsides, so carefully examine your objectives before going for your credit card. For example, if you want more traffic to your site, which will lead to more purchases, you must include strong commercial purpose keywords in your sponsored search techniques. Competition for these search keywords may be tough (and costly), but the rewards can be worthwhile.

Get Social

It is not enough to provide fantastic content and hopes that people will discover it; you must also be proactive. One of the most efficient ways to increase traffic to your website is to advertise it on social media networks. While Twitter is wonderful for short, snappy interactions, Google+

marketing may help your site appear in tailored search results and looks to be especially helpful in B2B regions. If you sell B2C items, image-heavy social networks such as Pinterest and Instagram might help you receive a lot of attention. Here are some more suggestions for making the most of social media marketing.

Contrary to common opinion, there is no one-size-fits-all formula for content marketing success. As a result, alter the length and structure of your material to appeal to as many various types of readers as feasible. For example, for optimal effect, mix short, news-based blog articles with long-form material, video, infographics, and data-driven pieces.

Write Irresistible Headlines

One of the essential aspects of your material is the headline. Even the most detailed blog article will go unread if it has an engaging headline. Learn how to write headlines. For example, authors at BuzzFeed and Upworthy may write up to twenty potential titles before settling on the one that would generate the most traffic, so think carefully about your headline before clicking "publish."

Target Long-Tail Keywords

Have you covered the basics for high-intent and popular keywords? Then it's time to concentrate on long-tail keywords. Long-tail keywords account for the majority of web searches, so if you're not targeting them as part of your sponsored search or SEO efforts, you're missing out.

Start Guest Blogging

Before you say anything, contrary to popular belief, real guest blogging is not extinct. On the contrary, obtaining a guest post on a reputable site may increase blog traffic to your website while also assisting in the growth of your brand. However, be aware that guest posting standards have evolved considerably in the previous eighteen months, and spamming tactics may result in severe penalties. Exercise great care.

When it comes to guest writing, it's a two-way street. In addition to providing material on other sites, invite individuals in your niche to post on your site. They are likely to share and link to their guest piece, bringing more viewers to your site. Just make sure you only submit high-quality, unique material free of spammy links since Google is cracking down on low-quality guest blogging.

Go After Referral Traffic

Instead of striving to persuade other websites to link back to you, create content that begs to be linked to.

When Larry wrote about how Google's Panda upgrade gave eBay a kick in the teeth, we could obtain a connection from Ars Technica in the Editor's Pick section, with links to The New York Times and National Geographic are two of the most well-known publications in the world. Not terrible, and neither was the rise in referral traffic as a result. Learn about the different sorts of links that deliver a lot of referral traffic and obtain them. Just be sure you concentrate on obtaining a steady flow of referral traffic from reliable sites. Otherwise, you may face a Google penalty.

Implement Schema Microdata

Implementing schema (or another microdata format) will not automatically increase traffic to your website, but it will make it easier for search engine bots to locate and index your content. Another advantage of adopting schema for SEO is that it can lead to better rich site snippets, increasing click-through rates.

Link Internally

The strength of your link profile is defined not only by the number of sites that link back to you but also by your internal linking structure. So keep an eye out for possibilities for internal links while producing and distributing material. This not only helps with SEO, but it also leads to a better, more helpful user experience - the foundation of boosting traffic to your website.

Interview Industry Thought Leaders

Think interviews are exclusively for the big leaguers? Think again. You'd be amazed how many people will talk to you if you just ask. Send out letters seeking interviews with industry thought leaders, and then post the interviews on your site. Not only will the name recognition improve your reputation and drive visitors to your website, but the interviewee will most likely share the material as well, extending its reach even further.

Make Sure Your Site is Responsive

The days of only browsing the internet on desktop computers are long gone. More people than ever before are accessing the web via mobile devices nowadays, and requiring your visitors to pinch and scroll their way through your site is practically begging them to leave. Therefore, even if you only have a simple website, you must guarantee that it is accessible and comfortable to browse various devices, including tiny smartphones.

Make Sure Your Site is Fast

Have you ever waited thirty seconds for a webpage to load? I don't either. If your site takes an eternity to load, your bounce rate will be exceedingly high. Ensure your pages are as technically optimized as feasible, including picture file sizes, page layout, and third-party plugin functioning. The more quickly your site loads, the better.

Foster a Sense of Community

People want to express themselves and weigh in on issues they are passionate about, so incorporating a community into your website is a fantastic way to start a dialogue and drive traffic to your site. Install a comprehensive commenting system using third-party solutions such as Facebook comments or Disqus, or build a separate forum where visitors may ask issues. However, remember to monitor your community to ensure that minimum standards of decency are met.

Make Yourself Heard in Comment Sections

You undoubtedly frequent at least a few sites related to your industry daily, so why not join the conversation? Of course, commenting may not always result in an instant increase in referral traffic. Still, creating a reputation for yourself by posting intelligent, thought-provoking comments on industry blogs and sites is a wonderful way to get your name out there, which can drive more traffic to your site. Remember that, as with guest posting, quality and relevance are essential - you should be connecting with others in your field rather than putting spam links on irrelevant websites.

Examine Your Analytics Data

Google Analytics is a goldmine of information on almost every element of your website, from your most popular pages to visitor demographics. Maintain vigilance over your Analytics data and utilize it to inform your advertising and content initiatives. First, keep track of which posts and pages are the most popular. Next, examine visitor statistics to determine where, how, and when your site's traffic is coming from.

Submit Your Content to Aggregator Sites

To begin, a disclaimer: don't spam Reddit and other similar sites in the hopes of "hitting the jackpot" of referral traffic because it won't happen. Members of communities like Reddit are quite alert to spam masquerading as real links. Still, it never hurts to contribute links that these audiences will find truly beneficial now and again. So choose a suitable subreddit, post your material, and then sit back and watch the traffic flood in.

Incorporate Video into Your Content Strategy

Text-based material is fine, but video can significantly draw new users and make your site more engaging. In addition, data demonstrate that visual content has much greater information retention than text, implying that video marketing is an effective method to capture – and retain – your audience's attention while also increasing traffic to your website.

Host Webinars

People enjoy learning, and webinars are a fantastic opportunity to share your knowledge with an interested audience. When combined with a strong social advertising effort, Webinars are an excellent method to drive visitors to your website. Send out an email around a week before the webinar, as well as a "last opportunity to register" reminder the day before. Make a point of saving the presentation for subsequent viewing and widely publicizing your webinars on social media. If you're wondering how to host a webinar, follow this link for some pointers.

Attend Conferences

Whatever sector you work in, there are likely to be at least one or two big conventions and conferences that are important to your company. It's a good idea to attend these events; speaking at them is even better. Even a mediocre speaking engagement is a fantastic opportunity to position oneself as an industry thought leader and receive substantial exposure for your website. I'd love to hear your suggestions for increasing traffic to your website.

Chapter-03: Other Free Ways to Increase Website Traffic

Get Listed in Online Directories

Another way to attract traffic to your website is to put it in free online directories and review sites. Because your profile on most of these sites will include a link to your website, frequently updating these listings and receiving favorable evaluations is likely to result in increased website traffic. Furthermore, several directories, such as Yelp, have high domain authority on Google. Therefore, there's a chance your company's free Yelp page may rank high for related searches.

Build Backlinks

A backlink is a link from another website to yours. For example, backlinks from comparable firms or industry leaders will not only expose your company to a broader audience but will also generate qualified traffic to your website.

Furthermore, Google detects backlinks and will boost its trust in your company if it notices other trustworthy websites referring to yours. More Google trust leads to higher ranks, which leads to more visitors. Quality backlinks will help you get recognized on Google for free.

Post to Social Media

Social networking is one of the most popular free marketing platforms available, and it may help drive visitors to your website. Use social media platforms such as Facebook, Instagram, and LinkedIn to promote blog articles and other helpful pages on your website. If you post shareable material, you may convert your social media followers into website visitors and drive traffic from their networks. Creating useful content is free and not as difficult as it may appear. You are the authority on your product or service; your duty is to make it understandable to your audience.

Include Hashtags in Your Posts

By including hashtags in articles promoting your website pages and blog posts, you may go beyond your network and be discovered by individuals searching for your products and services. The more people click on your links, the more free traffic you'll get to your website.

Use Landing Pages

Landing pages are yet another free way to drive visitors to your website. These are sites dedicated to your offerings, such as redeeming a coupon code, downloading a free guide, or beginning a free trial. They provide the information users require to proceed and convert and focus on one single call to action, increasing the likelihood that it will occur. Because landing pages are so precise, you can be very particular with your messaging, driving traffic (and conversions) to those pages.

Start Email Marketing

Sending out frequent newsletters and pushing deals via email is a wonderful method to remain in contact with your consumers while also increasing traffic to your website. Provide relevant information and connections to places on your website where customers may learn more, such as blog articles and landing pages for specific offers. Just make sure you aren't constantly bombarding your readers with emails, or they will disengage, delete, or unsubscribe from your emails. Also, pay close attention to the subject lines of your emails. These have a big influence on whether or not someone opens your email. Your emails will not drive visitors to your website if they are never opened!

Guest Blog

Having an industry influencer write a blog post and publish it on your site or converting an interview with them into a blog post may help increase traffic organically and by the influencer sharing the material with their audience. This might also assist in diversifying your material and demonstrate to your readers that you are active in your area. You may also ask the influencer to mention your firm in their review or round-up piece. This technique is still free, but it requires coordination with the influencer to be a mutually beneficial trade.

You may also contribute by serving as a guest blogger. Determine complimentary firms in your region whose target demographic is related to yours. See if you can write a piece for their blog that includes a link to your website. Make sure your material is relevant and valuable to their audience so that the trade is more equitable.

Learn from Your Analytics

Google Analytics is completely free to use, and the information it provides can help you generate more visitors to your website. Use tracked links in your marketing activities and monitored your website statistics regularly. This will allow you to determine which tactics and types of material work, which need to be improved, and which should be avoided.

Chapter-04: Paid Methods of Generating Website Traffic

Social network advertisements, display ads, and re-targeting ads are effective online advertising techniques for increasing website visitors.

Social Media Advertising

While search advertising pays to appear at the top of relevant search results, social media advertising pays to appear in relevant feeds. Both types of advertising allow you to define the audience in front of whom you want to appear, but social media enables superior targeting due to greater psychographic data.

Display Advertising

Display advertising is branded banner advertisements that appear on related websites. For example, if you are a fitness company and your ad is on a page regarding sports equipment, your ad will likely attract relevant traffic to your website. Ads for re-targeting might show on websites or in social media feeds. They are shown to visitors who have previously visited your site once and are thus more likely to return.

Avoid Instant Website Traffic Generators

There is such a thing as free-market website traffic, but no magic button or gadget creates it without your involvement. Here are three reasons to avoid using an automatic internet traffic generator for your business, whether paid or free.

Automatic Website Traffic Generators Can Be Harmful to Your Rankings

Google can identify spammy conduct, notices spikes in inactivity, and tracks how people interact with your website. However, using an automated traffic bot or generator is likely to attract the wrong type of attention from Google, harming your reputation and, as a result, your ranking.

Your traffic Won't Be Targeted

The ultimate objective is to increase the number of people who interact with your company by increasing visitors to your website and ranking higher on Google. If your consumers aren't targeted, they're less likely to connect with your website, lowering your lead and conversion rates.

Your Site Could Get Banned

If your website receives bot traffic, you risk being blocked from online advertising networks or, worse, being deleted from Google. Buying cheap website traffic is not worth it! Instead, take the effort to create high-quality, long-term traffic to your website.

As previously said, increasing traffic to your website is pointless if those users are unlikely to connect with your pages, convert into leads, or become customers. Increasing the number of visitors to your website does not happen overnight. It requires work, but the amount of effort you put in will be proportional to the quality of traffic you create. Plus, we've taken care of the difficult part for you: deciding what to do in the first place. You can obtain the proper people to your site and, more crucially, more of those visits to convert into buyers by using Google My Business and the other secure routes described above.

Google Paid Ways to Drive Website Traffic

Paid Google advertising is an excellent method to get visitors to your website looking for the services you offer.

Google Ads

You pay Google Ads to have your website (typically a landing page) appear at the top of search results for specific keywords. When a query using such keywords is submitted, Google examines all accounts bidding on those keywords and displays and ranks the paid results based on the quality and relevancy of the advertising.

Paid search results appear first, at the top of the results pages. This sort of exposure is an excellent method to get more quality visitors to your website. But, of course, you also only pay when someone clicks on your ad.

Google Maps Advertising

You may also set settings through the Google Ads network to have your company appear at the top of Google Maps search results. As with typically paid search advertising, there will be a notice next to your listing indicating a sponsored result, but the visibility gained by being at the top is priceless.

Chapter-05: Increase Website Traffic from Google

Why More Website Traffic?

Some companies ask whether it is even necessary to have a website in the first place. In today's environment, even brick-and-mortar companies must have a website. At the very least, potential consumers will get more acquainted with your company. However, it should be structured so that people may enter your funnel and finally convert it into clients.

Your website's traffic is a vital indicator and a driver of business success when you use this sort of website. It can be of use to you in the following ways:
- Examine the efficacy of your marketing.
- Gather information about your target audience before making a choice.
- Improve the trustworthiness of your SEO and search engine results.
- Increase the number of leads generated, conversion rates, and clients acquired.

Free Traffic vs. Quality Traffic

Traffic to your website helps enhance your rank, which produces more traffic, but you must ensure that an increase in interaction accompanies the rise in traffic. If your traffic is rising, but your conversion rates are declining, you are not attracting the proper visitors. There are several strategies to optimize your website for conversions. These include placing calls to action and lead capture forms in strategic locations, giving the information your visitors need, and making navigation simple and intuitive. The first step, though, is to get the proper people to your site in the first place. When it comes to website traffic, your objective is to generate more quality users for your site. Those who are most likely to become leads or clients.

Quality Traffic Driven Channels to Your Website

No one-and-done method can create free and high-quality website traffic to your website. Rather, there is a combination of channels that work in tandem to generate visits. Some need effort, while others necessitate time and money. The following are some of the techniques and channels that attract visitors to your website:
- Online Directory Listings
- On-Page SEO
- Off-Page SEO
- Email
- Social Media
- Online Ads
- Blogging

In the next part, we'll go through the most efficient (and dependable) techniques to increase website traffic for free. There are a few strategies you may utilize Google to enhance the traffic to your website.

Optimize Your Free Google Business Profile

Did you know that a properly optimized Google business listing receives seven times the amount of visitors as a non-optimized one? Also, remember that your listing includes a connection to your website, which is an excellent method to increase visitors to your website.

Keep in mind that Google's results pages are becoming increasingly intelligent. Therefore, if your listing has all of the information a potential client requires to make a choice, they may bypass your website and contact/visit your business directly – which is preferable to a website visit!

Here are some more Google My Business features and perks that make it one of the finest sources of excellent website traffic.

Your Google listing
- It is free and simple to start up.
- Allows you to appear in searches related to your business and location.
- Increases your visibility on a platform where consumers are interested in purchasing.
- Brings quality visitors to your website and shop.
- Allows consumers to provide reviews, which helps to increase your visibility.

Keep in mind, too, that Google My Business:
- Allows your company to be found in mobile searches, which have overtaken desktop searches.
- Uses images to give customers a feel of what it's like to work at your company, reducing ambiguity, which is a key barrier to entry.

- Allows searchers to interact with your company straight from your listing, boosting interaction possibilities and acquiring new clients.

Given the numerous advantages of having a Google My Business listing, you can't afford to have one as a local business. CreaSo creator listing and keep it

Perform On-Page SEO

You may use several SEO strategies on each of your website's pages to improve their ranking in search engines and attract more users. This involves creating high-quality content that your target audience is looking for and generating succinct meta descriptions for your sites. In search results, the meta description shows beneath your URL. Knowing what a page is about and what will happen in a click increases the likelihood of users clicking. On-page SEO methods like these are free, but they do require time.

Chapter-06: Increase Website Traffic via social media

Start a podcast

Fifty-one percent of Americans have listened to a podcast, 32 percent listening at least once a month. So podcasts have a large audience, and establishing one to promote your online brand can increase visitors to your site.

Podcasting can help you in a variety of ways:
- Users may find you first through your podcast and then visit your website to learn more.
- Nurture customer connections by providing more value to your consumers with podcast content. You might even include an interactive component to provide consumers with a more personalized brand experience.
- SEO: By transcribing your podcasts, you may embed the audio and upload the text to your website's blog, providing more opportunities to optimize for search.

Write on Medium

Medium is a blogging platform where individuals and businesses publish blog articles with basic HTML and CSS editing and style. The site has also developed a community of publishers who can follow, interact with, and promote the works of others. You may present your business to this preexisting community. You will get momentum and readers after investing resources in building a fantastic content experience on Medium. You may entice readers to your online store by providing links back to your site.

Master YouTube marketing

Create YouTube advertisements, add links to your description, add annotation links to your video, or encourage other YouTubers to post your links on their videos to enhance Traffic from YouTube. You will be able to attract more visitors back to your website if you create a new video at least once a week, regularly, and overtime. If you don't have an audience yet, you may approach YouTubers with huge followings and ask them to become paying their fee. This may work in the near term, but it is always a good idea to build out your channels to reduce acquisition expenses.

Increase website traffic with LinkedIn

LinkedIn appears to be the last site you'd expect to gain visitors from for most online shops. Even if it isn't your first focus, you may still obtain a regular stream of visitors from this source. Many internet shops utilize LinkedIn to disseminate press releases. For example, if you just gave to a charity, wish to recognize a team member, or reached a major milestone for your company, you might publish an article from your website on LinkedIn. Sharing product URLs is unusual unless the product is a first-of-its-kind. In terms of views and interaction, videos do exceptionally well on LinkedIn. You might improve website traffic by including a link to your website in a post containing a video.

Add social share buttons

Add social share buttons to shareable pages on your website, such as blog posts, product pages and pictures, and other material. These social share buttons make it simple for visitors to share your content (complete with links!), providing you with social proof and traffic. When their network sees these postings, they can visit your website. For example, the skincare brand Speak includes social sharing buttons beneath product descriptions and above user reviews on its product websites.

Engage in email marketing

You'll be able to maintain generating internet traffic to your business with email marketing as long as your consumers are enrolled. With social media platforms constantly limiting your reach, email marketing is one of the few marketing methods you have total control over.

Building a list for email marketing might take a long time, so get started right now. You may develop an email list by including Email Pirate on your website, which adds opt-in forms. You may also utilize Spin-a-Sale to gather emails based on exit intent or try product Notify, which sends emails to consumers when the price of a product changes.

Maximize Twitter marketing

While Twitter has cracked down on spam automation, you may still use this traffic source. If you're still learning how to boost website traffic, Twitter is a wonderful place to start. You won't have to be concerned about a lack of reach. You might reach a larger audience than your following count by using relevant hashtags.

When it comes to content marketing, a simple method for increasing Twitter traffic is to share a click-to-retweet link with persons mentioned in the post. This increases the exposure of your initial tweet, especially if it contains a hashtag because it can help you rank higher in the stream for the hashtag used. Consequently, more eyes will be drawn to the tweet, and your website will have a greater click-through rate.

Check out Pinterest

Pinterest is one of the most effective strategies to increase website traffic. Pinterest traffic might surpass powerhouses like Facebook if you post your items and blog material many times each week. Then, it just takes one viral pin to send an infinite flood of traffic to your website.

You may pin all of the photos in a blog post if you're sharing it. This provides you with numerous possibilities for a pin to take off – one of your images may outshine the others. As a consequence, you may be able to attract even more visitors to your website. For example, assume you wish to publicize a product page. If the product photographs on that page aren't exciting, you may submit unique images to lure visits to your website. You may try the Binoculars app, which re-targets Pinterest visitors, to improve website traffic from Pinterest.

Try influencer marketing

Influencers may be used in a variety of ways to increase site traffic:

- Pay influencers to post about your company and products on social media, including links.
- Persuade influencers to include you in their email newsletters.
- Create connections with influential bloggers so that they will mention your brand on their blog.
- Send complimentary items to influencers and ask them to provide an honest review on their networks.
- Get your name included in influencer round-up articles.
- Identify influencers in your material and share the links with them as a "Hey, I wrote about you!" – people enjoy free publicity and may be ready to spread it with their networks.

Reach out to affiliates

Affiliate marketing is a type of marketing in which businesses pay affiliates to promote their products. Affiliates are paid a portion of the income generated by each sale they refer to. These purchases are frequently generated through internet visits. Perhaps the affiliate is a blogger or social media influencer who shares a link with their referral or tracking code. You pay the affiliate the agreed-upon fee each time someone uses that code to make a transaction.

Advertise via ad networks

If you have a budget, take advantage of the possibility provided by ad networks. Create digital advertising that promotes your website, tailor them to your ideal consumer, and then sit back and watch the traffic pour in.
Check out the following ad networks:
- Google Display Network

- AdRoll
- Microsoft Advertising
- Quora ads
- Taboola
- Outbrain

Only 2% of visitors will make a purchase the first time they visit your website. Therefore, Re-targeting advertisements are particularly powerful because you're selling to a warm audience, hoping to get them to return for a second visit. As a result, you will have an easier job persuading them to convert.

The conversion in the case of re-targeting advertisements is the click-through to your site.

Optimize your best traffic source

Examine your data to determine your greatest traffic source. Consider the following factors while determining the best sources:

- Which sources provide the most traffic?
- Which sources generate the most high-converting traffic?
- Which sources generate the most active traffic?

Then, figure out why certain sources are so effective. Then go for it twice as hard. This is referred to as optimization.

Conclusion

You've picked a fantastic product and designed a fantastic store. All you have to do now is find out how to generate visitors to your website so that sales may flow in. These suggestions will help you figure out what it takes to discover how to boost internet traffic in your shop, from social media to unconventional marketing techniques. You'll also learn what pros use to boost traffic to their websites. We'll also include some website traffic checker tools so you can see how much traffic you're getting and where it's coming from. Don't sit around waiting for someone else to do it. Hire yourself and start making decisions. Consider basing re-targeting advertisements on user behavior to attract more visitors to your site. Automations may be triggered depending on online activities, allowing you to create a more personalized and engaging experience.

www.ingramcontent.com/pod-product-compliance
Lightning Source LLC
Chambersburg PA
CBHW030039230526
45472CB00002B/589